Published in Great Britain in MMXVII by
Book House, an imprint of
The Salariya Book Company Ltd
25 Marlborough Place, Brighton BN1 1UB
www.salariya.com

ISBN: 978-1-910706-67-1

SALARIYA

A CIP catalogue record for this book is available
from the British Library.

Printed and bound in China.

DRAGONFLY

Louise & Richard
Spilsbury

UP CLOSE &
SCARY

BOOK HOUSE
a SALARIYA imprint

Contents

Dragonflies

Dragonflies are large, winged **insects** that can be seen flying near water. They are harmless to humans, although big dragonflies can nip if you hold them. Dragonflies are a fearsome **predator** of flying insects and other small animals, such as fish. They glide over water or dart about, grabbing **prey** quickly from the air.

Dragonflies are such efficient killers that they capture more than nine out of every ten animals that they target. This is an impressive record that other predators would envy. A shark catches only about half of the prey it hunts, and a lion catches around one-quarter of its prey.

Some adult dragonflies live for just a few weeks but others can live for up to a year.

Dragonflies are one of the deadliest predators on the planet.

Dragonflies were some of the first winged insects on Earth, around 300 million years ago. They were much bigger and scarier than dragonflies today because they had **wingspans** of up to 60 cm (2 feet) wide.

The body

Like all insects, the dragonfly has six legs and a body made up of three main parts: head, **thorax** and **abdomen**. The thorax is very strong and full of **muscles**. It controls the head, wing and leg movements. The abdomen is long and thin. It gives the dragonfly its characteristic shape. Dragonflies breathe through holes in the abdomen and **digest** food there.

Superpowers

Some female dragonflies have a sharp tool with saw-like edges at the end of their abdomen. It is called an **ovipositor**. They use the ovipositor to cut slits in the stems or leaves of water plants so that they can lay their eggs inside. Imagine if humans had a body part that could work like a chainsaw to cut up trees.

8

Head

Thorax

Dragonfly thoraxes are often striped.

Like other insects, the dragonfly's body is supported by a hard **exoskeleton**.

The abdomen is made up of ten segments so that the dragonfly can bend and curl it up.

Ovipositor

9

The head

A dragonfly's head is round. It perches at the end of the dragonfly's neck so that it can swivel around easily. The dragonfly's huge eyes take up most of the head. The two bristly **antennae** are small and can be difficult to see. They are **sense organs**. They help the dragonfly to measure the speed and direction of the wind so that it can chase its victims in the air.

Superpowers

A dragonfly's huge, bulging eyes give it a 360-degree view of the world. Dragonflies can see forwards and backwards, and above and underneath themselves to spot prey and predators, such as birds, fish, frogs and lizards. If humans had eyes like these, they would wrap around their head like an astronaut's helmet. They would then be able to see in all directions.

10

Eyes

Dragonfly eyes are so big that they often touch at the top of the head.

The antennae are small because dragonflies rely more on their eyes to find prey.

Some dragonflies use their huge eyes to help them to hunt at dusk when there is little light.

The eyes

The dragonfly's two **compound eyes** give it excellent eyesight. It uses its eyes to find and catch small insects in the air and to spot predators. A dragonfly sees movements as if they are in slow motion. For example it can see the separate beats of an insect's rapidly beating wings, which look like a blur to humans.

Superpowers

Each dragonfly eye is made up of almost 30,000 individual *facets*. Each facet contains a tiny *lens*. The dragonfly brain combines thousands of images from the lenses into one whole image. Dragonflies can see *ultraviolet (UV) light*, which is invisible to the human eye, and colours far beyond the range that humans can normally see.

12

The many facets of the compound eyes are packed side by side into a tight honeycomb formation.

Each facet points in a slightly different direction, to give the dragonfly a wide field of view.

Dragonflies also have three smaller eyes called ocelli.

The ocelli can detect movement more quickly than the huge compound eyes can.

A dragonfly's eyes help it to target a single animal within a swarm, while at the same time, it can see the rest of the insects to avoid crashing into them.

The mouth

A dragonfly often eats its dinner in mid-air without stopping to land. One reason it can do this is because its **hinged** jaws can open as wide as its entire head, allowing the dragonfly to eat almost anything smaller than it is. When a dragonfly catches an insect, its jagged jaws clamp down hard and rip the prey's wings so that it cannot escape. The dragonfly quickly chews its victim into a gooey pulp and swallows it.

Superpowers

Dragonflies never seem to stop eating. They can eat hundreds of flies every day. Some dragonflies regularly eat animals that are 60 percent of their own body weight. That would be like a person eating more than 30 meals in one sitting!

14

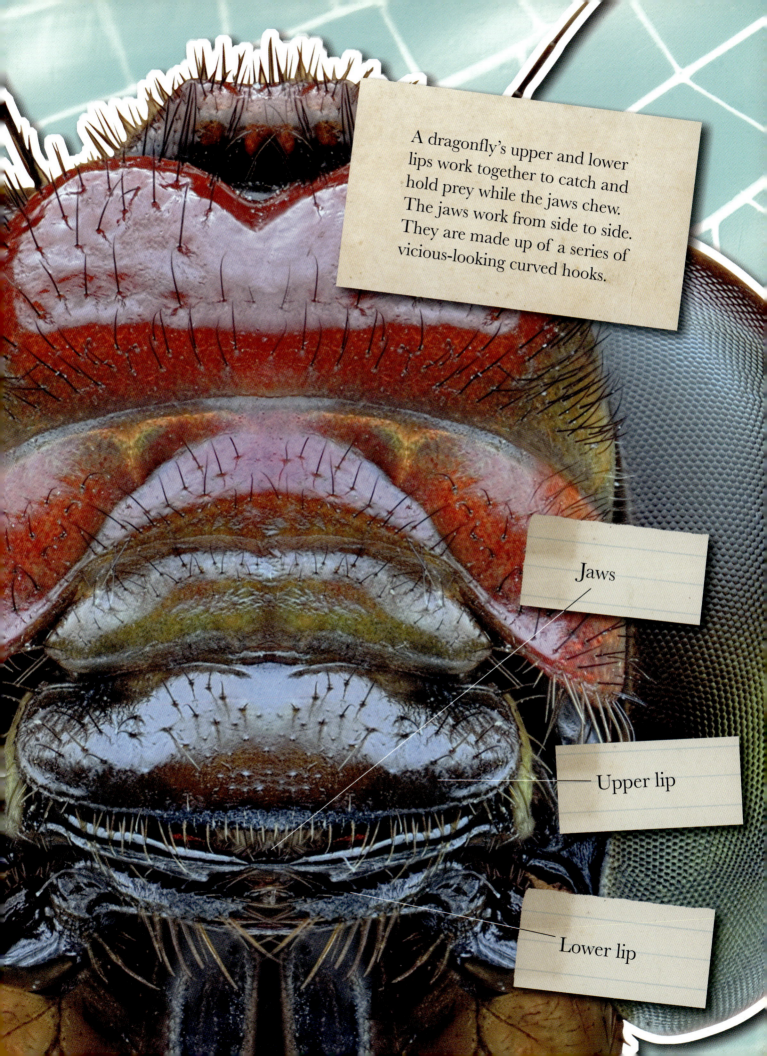

A dragonfly's upper and lower lips work together to catch and hold prey while the jaws chew. The jaws work from side to side. They are made up of a series of vicious-looking curved hooks.

Jaws

Upper lip

Lower lip

The wings

Dragonflies have two sets of transparent wings that often have coloured markings. Most dragonflies have a wingspan from 5 to 13 centimetres (2 to 5 inches). Dragonflies can beat each pair of wings together or separately. They can also move their back wings at a different rate from the front wings.

The largest dragonflies have a wingspan of up to 15 cm (6 in).

The **veins** that run through each wing give the wing strength and flexibility.

The lower wings are usually shorter and wider than the upper wings.

Superpowers

A dragonfly does not just fly forwards. It can change direction in mid-air and fly left and right or backwards. It can also hover on the spot. This is because its wings can beat and twist independently of each other, rather like a helicopter's blades. Just imagine if humans could take off straight up into the air and fly in all directions!

In flight

A dragonfly can fly further, higher and faster than most other insects when on the attack. A dragonfly does not just follow its victim but works out its prey's speed and direction, so that it can intercept it in mid-air. To avoid being seen, a dragonfly attacks from below. The dragonfly keeps its head still with its eyes locked onto its target, while its body gets into the best position to attack.

The wings of a dragonfly beat at up to 35 times a second.

Superpowers

A dragonfly is only 8 cm (3 in) long but it can fly through the air at about 35 kph (22 mph). An average adult man is about 6 feet tall. If he could run as fast as a dragonfly can fly, he would zoom past at almost 900 kph (560 mph)!

The dragonfly's thorax is packed with muscles for moving the wings up and down and side to side.

Its long abdomen keeps its body balanced while manoeuvring through the air.

The dragonfly is the aerial stunt artist of the insect world. Each of their four wings is controlled by different muscles, so they have perfect control over their flight.

19

The legs

Dragonflies have six legs but they cannot walk on solid ground. They use their legs to grab their prey while flying, and to perch and balance on plants so that they can rest or feed on very large prey. Dragonflies also use their legs for grooming. Their legs have bristles that they can use like combs to rub cobwebs, dust and water off their eyes and abdomen.

Superpowers

To catch prey, a dragonfly curves up its front legs and scoops the insect out of the air as it flies past. The bristles that cover its legs form a net to catch the insect, and a cage to trap the prey, cutting off its escape. If humans could use the hairs on their arms as giant nets, they would be able to catch and carry anything they liked.

20

Dragonflies put their legs forward to grasp vertical plant stems when they come into land. They also use their legs to catch prey.

Claw

Each of the dragonfly's legs is **jointed** so that the dragonfly can bend and curl its limbs.

Bristles

A dragonfly uses the claws at the end of each of its legs to grip its prey.

21

Nymphs

Dragonfly **larvae** are called nymphs. The nymphs hatch from eggs underwater and live in the water for a year or more. The nymphs are just as scary as their parents. They catch and eat anything that they can fit in their mouths, from small insects to tadpoles and small fish. As they grow, the nymphs **moult** many times to shed their hard, outer skin. Finally, they crawl out of the water and moult one last time, emerging as an adult dragonfly with wings.

Superpowers

Nymphs breathe by taking water into their abdomen and through body parts called **gills**. They can also squeeze a jet of this water out through the end of their abdomen to make themselves shoot through the water at high speed. If humans had built-in jetpacks like these, they could shoot through the water like torpedoes!

Mandibles

Jaw

Mouth

Dragonfly nymphs have a long, hinged jaw with two sharp, hook-like mandibles at the end. The mandibles shoot forward and impale prey on the hooks, then pull it back into the mouth to eat it.

Green darners

There are about 5,000 different **species**, or types, of dragonfly. The common green darner is one of the largest species. It grows up to about 8 cm (3 in) long. Green darners can **migrate** thousands of miles from northern USA into Texas and Mexico. They travel south to lay their eggs in warmer places. These dragonflies are scary predators, capable of killing a hummingbird.

The bright green head, thorax and abdomen of this dragonfly **camouflage** it against plants.

The green darner's wings are clear but they turn a honey-yellow colour as they get older.

Superpowers

Female common green darners can disappear! Well, not completely, but when they stop flying and land on a plant, they are almost impossible to see. Their green and brown body blends in with the leaves and stems, providing them with camouflage that hides them from hungry predators. If humans could blend in with a background, they too could disappear whenever they wanted.

The green darner sometimes turns a greyish or even purple colour when it gets cold. Scientists think that this helps it to absorb more warmth from the sun.

The green darner is named for its very long, thin abdomen that looks like a darning needle.

Dragonhunters

Dragonhunters are as scary to dragonflies as they are to other prey. They are vicious predators that feed on other dragonflies, as well as butterflies and other large insects. Their abdomen has a very large end, known as the 'club', which is usually larger in the male than in the female. These dragonflies are often brown or black, with yellow or green markings for camouflage.

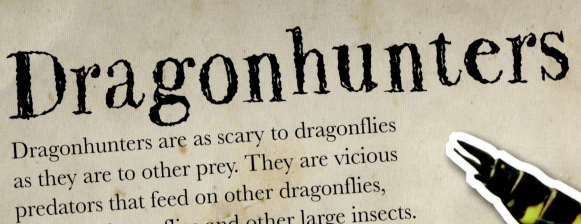

Club

Superpowers

Some scientists believe that dragonhunters use their club to mimic scorpions or tree snakes to scare off predators. If humans had this superpower, they could pretend to be scarier people or animals to keep themselves out of harm's way.

Large body

The dragonhunter is a monster dragonfly! It grows to more than 9 cm (3.5 in) long.

Small head

Long, powerful legs and wings

27

That's scary!

Dragonflies are perfect killing machines but that is not the scariest thing about them. The truly scary thing about dragonflies is that some species are dying out, which is bad news for people.

Some species are dying out because there are fewer **wetland habitats** as people fill in ponds and lakes to build houses or to create farmland. **Pollution** and farm chemicals, such as **insecticides**, also kill dragonflies. Dragonflies are very sensitive to changes in temperature, so they will not be able to survive heatwaves or heavy rains that may come with **climate change**.

Dragonflies help people in important ways. They are amazing pest controllers because they eat so many mosquitoes and other biting insects. Not only can biting insects be annoying but some also spread deadly diseases. For example, mosquitoes spread malaria, which kills hundreds of thousands of people each year. Dragonflies also eat aphids, which are tiny insects that can destroy crops and other plants.

Dragonflies are important and valuable insects because they help to control populations of harmful insects around the world.

Dragonflies might look scary close up but these beautiful insects are our friends, not our foes.

A dragonfly can eat hundreds of mosquitoes in a single day.

Glossary

Abdomen stomach.

Antennae sense organs located near the front of an insect's head.

Camouflage an animal's natural colouring or shape, which allows it to blend in with its surroundings.

Climate change the gradual increase in the Earth's temperature, thought to be caused by human actions, such as burning oil, gas and coal.

Compound eyes eyes made up of many lenses.

Digest to break down food to be absorbed into the body.

Exoskeleton the hard, outer covering on the outside of an animal's body.

Facet a small, smooth, flat surface.

Gills the body parts that dragonfly nymphs, fish and some other animals use to breathe underwater.

Habitats the places where an animal or plant usually lives.

Hinged joined in such a way that it opens and closes like a door.

Insects animals with six legs and a body divided into three sections: head, thorax, and abdomen. Some insects also have wings.

Insecticides a spray intended to kill the insects that harm crops and plants grown for food.

Jointed parts joined in a way that they can move separately, like the knee joint on a human leg.

Larvae the wingless, often wormlike, form of insects when first hatched from eggs.

Lens the part of an eye that gathers light so an animal can see.

Mandibles jaws.

Migrate to move from one place to another in different seasons.

Moult to shed hair or skin.

Muscles the parts of the body that can make an animal move.

Ovipositor a body part that female insects use to lay eggs.

Pollution something found in water, air or land that damages it or makes it harmful to living things.

Predator an animal that hunts other animals to eat.

Prey an animal that is hunted and eaten by other animals.

Sense organs body parts that give an animal one or more of the five senses. The five senses are sight, hearing, smell, taste and touch.

Species a type of animal or plant.

Thorax the chest or part of an animal's body between its head and its abdomen.

Ultraviolet (UV) light a form of light energy that humans cannot see.

Veins tubes in an animal's body that carry blood.

Wetland land saturated by water most or all of the time, such as a swamp, marsh, pond or lake.

Wingspan the total width of the wings from the tip of one wing to the tip of the other.

Index